REVISED AND UPDATED

Art In History

MAY - - 2009

DISCARD

Native American Art

Petra Press

Heinemann Library
Chicago, Illinois

© 2001, 2006 Heinemann Library
a division of Reed Elsevier Inc.
Chicago, Illinois

Customer Service 888-454-2279
Visit our website at www.heinemannraintree.com

Design by Victoria Bevan, Michelle Lisseter, and Q2A Media
Illustrations by Oxford Illustrators
Printed and bound in Hong Kong by WKT

10 09 08 07 06
10 9 8 7 6 5 4 3 2 1

New edition ISBNs: 1 40348 769 3 (hardback)
                     1 40348 777 4 (paperback)

The Library of Congress has cataloged the first edition as follows:
Press, Petra.
  Native American art / Petra Press.
    p. cm. -- (Art in history)
Includes bibliographical references and index.
  ISBN 1-58810-092-8 (HC), 1-4034-4020-4 (Pbk.)
  1. Indian art--North America--Juvenile literature. [1. Indian
art--North America.] I. Title. II. Series: Art in history (Chicago,
Ill.)
E98.A7 P74 2001
704.03'97--dc21
                        00-012481

Acknowledgments
The publishers would like to thank the following for permission to reproduce photographs:
© Corbis/David Muench, Cover; © Art Resource/Werner Forman p. 5; © Corbis/Morton Beebe, S.F. p. 6; © Corbis/Buddy Mays p. 7; © Corbis/Richard Hamilton Smith p. 8; © Corbis/David Muench p. 9; © American Museum Natural History/Neg./Transparency No. 319175. Courtesy Department of Library Services p. 10; © National Museum of American Art/Smithsonian American Art Museum, Gift of Mrs. Joseph Harrison, Jr. p. 11; © Corbis/Richard A Cooke p. 12; © Art Resource/Werner Forman Archive, Private Collection p. 13; © Brooklyn Museum/"Panther Effigy Pipe," USA, Indiana, AD 1–4000 Black steatite 6.0 x 17.t x 4.0 cm, Anonymous loan L49.5 p. 14; © Ohio Historical Society p. 15; © Art Resource/The Newark Museum, Newark, New Jersey p. 16; © Art Resource/Werner Forman Archive, Museum of Anthropology, University of British Columbia, Canada p. 17; © National Museum of the American Indian p. 18; © Portland Art Museum/Portland Art Museum, Portland, Oregon, Axel Rasmussen Collection, purchased with the Indian Collection Subscription Fund p. 19; © Corbis/Richard A Cooke p. 20; © Corbis/David Muench p. 21; © National Museum of the American Indian/Courtesy, National Museum of the American Indian, Smithsonian Institution (Neg# 15/0855) Photo by David Heald p. 22; © Art Resource/Werner Forman Archive, British Museum, London p. 23; © Corbis/Ted Spiegel p. 24; © Corbis/Buddy Mays p. 25; © Photo Researchers, Inc./Georg Gerster p. 26; © Saint Louis Art Musuem/Eliza McMillan Fund p. 27; © Bernice Steinbaum Gallery/Jeff Sturges p. 28.

Cover photograph of a button blanket reproduced with permission of Werner Forman Archive/University Museum, Pennsylvania.

The paper used to print this book comes from sustainable resources.

Contents

Some words are shown in bold, **like this**.
You can find out what they mean by looking in the glossary.

WHAT IS NATIVE AMERICAN ART?

Native American cultures have existed in North America for thousands of years. Over 500 different Native American nations were spread over seven major geographic areas, which are sometimes called **culture areas**. These areas are now called the Northwest Pacific Coast, California, Basin Plateau, Southwest, Great Plains, Southeast, and Eastern Woodlands. Each of these nations has a rich culture that is thousands of years old and includes history, government, religion, and myths.

Communities of Native North Americans developed artistic skills to express their beliefs and history in a variety of ways, just as people did in other parts of the world. The beautiful objects that Native Americans created always had a social or religious use. Creating art and practicing religion were part of everyday life, since **functional** objects were designed to remind people of their beliefs, their traditions, and their history.

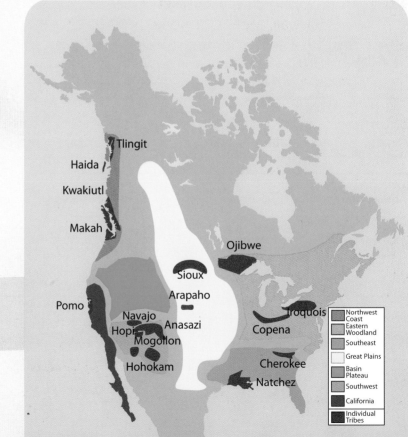

This map shows the different culture areas in North America.

Painting of a battle, Lakota Sioux, buckskin

Paintings like this one were often done to show the owner's skill in battle. The paintings were also used as historical documents that told people about their history and heroes.

Each culture developed a unique and recognizable style, although neighboring communities often traded skills and materials. Everyone created functional art objects. Since some people were more skilled than others, every type of art had specialists. Whether it was carving a **ceremonial** pipe, weaving a basket or blanket, or painting a battle scene on a rock wall, each artist worked very carefully to make the object contribute to the harmony and beauty of the world.

New tools and designs

Until the arrival of European settlers, Native Americans used painstaking traditional techniques to create their functional and ceremonial art objects. The Europeans introduced chemical dyes, the potter's wheel, metalworking, and the sewing needle, making it easier for Native Americans to produce some of their art. Europeans had a negative impact as well. Early European settlers wanted to trade for Native American pottery, baskets, and textiles (types of cloth), but they thought the designs were primitive (not skilled). Over the years, many Native American artists began to change the color, shape, and size of their creations to meet the demands of white traders.

SIGNS AND SYMBOLS

While no two Native American cultures developed exactly the same religion, most agreed that spirits lived in the animals, rocks, rivers, land, and trees around them. Every being had a soul that had to be respected. When a hunter killed a deer for food, he thanked the animal for its **sacrifice** and then buried its bones. This burial was meant to allow the deer's spirit to be reborn.

Native Americans believed that all life should be in harmony with its environment. **Shamans** held rituals to call on certain spirits to heal sickness and to protect the community from its enemies. Shamans carved and painted special masks, pipes, **rattles**, and **amulets** in the shapes of the spirits whose help they needed. Tlingit shamans in the Northwest Pacific Coast culture area asked the sea otter for help, while shamans in the Plains culture area called on the buffalo.

Totem poles were carved from one large tree trunk. Each animal spirit carved on the pole had a specific meaning and importance for the owner.

Totem pole, Kwakiutl people, British Columbia, cedar wood

Other tribe members carved amulets that they carried for protection against enemies and sickness. Often the person also carried an amulet in the shape of his or her animal spirit. The animal spirits and natural world are important symbols in Native American art.

Teenage boys spent months preparing for a **vision quest**. This was a **spiritual** event that sent the teenager on a long hike away from the village with no food and water. The teenager would stay away from the village until an animal came to him in a dream. He then took the animal spirit's name, such as Running Deer or Spotted Eagle, as his own, and returned to the village as an adult. Bears, deer, wolves, birds, and frogs all served as animal spirits.

Kachina, Hopi people, Arizona, wood

The Hopi believe that kachina carvings (see below) can pass on some of the power of the spirits they represent.

Kachinas

Hopi dancers wore carved and painted wooden masks in a ceremony to thank spirits, called kachinas, for a good harvest. Small kachina dolls were intricately carved from one piece of wood or one piece of the root of a cotton plant. Then, they were brightly painted. Kachinas were given to babies as amulets to bring good health and a long life.

ROCK ART

Pictograph, Hegman Lake, Minnesota, red paint on rock

This pictograph shows a hunter with his prey.

The pictures painted or carved on rocks or cave walls are called rock art. Rock art was used to record battles, history, and other important tribal events. Some cultures used it to tell religious stories. Over 2,500 years ago, the Anasazi Indians of the Southwest culture area painted human figures called **pictographs** on the sandstone rock of desert canyons, while the Great Plains people painted pictographs in the Midwest, near the Great Lakes. Painted in bright yellows and reds, the pictures showed people hunting animals or fighting each other. Many showed people playing flutes and other musical instruments. The most common paintings are red and white handprints of children and adults. They are believed to have been placed there during religious ceremonies.

Petroglyphs

The rock art found throughout the rest of North America was created over 1,000 years later. In addition to pictograph paintings of animal spirits, some cultures used a different kind of rock art, called **petroglyphs**. Petroglyphs were images or a kind of picture alphabet carved into rock. Petroglyphs recorded a tribe's history, served as a symbol in important ceremonies, or made detailed maps of hunting locations. These forms of rock art are important. By examining them, we can learn a lot about the way people used to live.

A shaman probably carved this figure during a ceremony, to ensure a successful hunt.

Petroglyph, Wind River Range, Wyoming, carving on rock

USING TREES AND PLANTS

Native Americans of the Eastern Woodlands culture area used the bark of white birch trees to make hundreds of useful objects. The bark was light, easy to work with, waterproof, and did not rot in hot weather. This made it perfect for constructing canoes and covering **wigwams**. People also made storage containers out of it and used it to make hunting and fishing gear, musical instruments, decorative fans, and even children's sleds and other toys. Birch bark was also used to write on, since it is durable (strong) and light enough to be carried around.

Records, Ojibwe people, birch bark, c. 1600s

These records are easily readable, even after being handled by many people. They were made by Ojibwe people, who were part of the Midewiwin group. This was a secret society of shamans. It was formed to protect people from new diseases that had been brought by the European settlers. The members kept notes about their meetings on birch bark.

Portrait of an Iroquois
Wife, *George Catlin, c. 1835*

This Iroquois woman has made
a cradle for her baby using
branches and plant fibers.

Native Americans also used the roots and twigs of willow, spruce, and
pine trees, as well as plants such as cattail and corn husks, to create
household objects, bows and arrows, children's toys and cradles, and
ceremonial masks and rattles. People could easily bend plant fibers
into many different shapes. Plant fibers gave the finished objects
interesting textures and colors.

WOOD SCULPTURE

Wood carving was especially popular along the Northwest Pacific Coast culture area. Here, people cut large planks from trees to construct houses big enough to hold dozens of people. They built canoes that were large enough to hunt whales out on the ocean. They also carved tall poles decorated with their family's totems and guardian animal spirits. They carved helmets, shields, and clubs to use in battle. Almost all of their carved objects, whether large or small, were richly painted. Paint was made from bark, berries, and moss. The artists painted the carving using a paintbrush made of porcupine hair.

Carved wood rattle, Makah people, Washington

Rattles like this one were used in religious ceremonies or to emphasize parts of important speeches.

The potlatch

Northwest Pacific Coast people were able to store much of the food that they hunted, fished, and gathered in the summers. This allowed them to devote their winters to throwing elaborate feasts and parties called **potlatches**. It was traditional to give each of one's guests a beautifully carved or woven gift. The more elaborate the gifts, the higher one's status in the community. The gifts were often beautifully carved serving bowls or intricately designed blankets.

Wood carving was also a highly developed skill in the heavily forested Eastern Woodlands culture areas. People living in and near forests used wood for just about everything, including tool handles, containers to store food and clothing, ceremonial masks and rattles, serving bowls, and utensils, such as spoons and corn flatteners. They often carved these items into the shapes of beavers, hawks, snakes, and other animals.

In the Southeast culture area, mask carving was a highly developed speciality. The Cherokee carved cougar masks for ceremonies to honor the cougar and to give the hunters cat-like hunting abilities. They also carved masks for ceremonies like the Boogerman Dance, a dance that was performed to scare away evil spirits that tried to harm their crops. They painted and decorated the wooden masks with animal fur, quills, feathers, toenails, and even teeth.

Masks like this one were used in elaborate ceremonial dances. Kwakiutl masks had parts that could move for more dramatic ceremonies.

Mask of a beaver and killer whale, Kwakiutl people, British Columbia, c. AD 1700

BASKETRY

Native Americans in the Great Plains and the Southwest were weaving baskets over 11,000 years ago. The Anasazi, **ancestors** of the Pueblo people in the Southwest culture area, used baskets for everything from baby cradles to funeral jars. They also used baskets to gather and store food. They wove bowl-shaped baskets so tightly that they were waterproof. They used these baskets as hats or to transport water. They could also use them to cook food.

During the 1800s, the Pomo people made coiled baskets like this one to sell to white settlers in California. They sold the baskets to raise money to help buy back their land from the white settlers.

Pomo ceremonial gift basket, Pomo people, California, willow, feathers, abalone shells, c. 1800s

Basket with killer whale design, Tlingit people, Alaska, woven spruce root

Baskets like this one were useful as well as beautiful. This basket is woven, not coiled.

Weaving and coiling

There were two major ways to make baskets: weaving and coiling. Both ways used many types of grasses, roots, bark, and other plant materials. Weaving (pulling softer fibers in and out of stiffer fibers that formed the basic basket shape) produced the strongest baskets. Coiling (wrapping a long, thick strand of fiber around and around and then sewing the coils together) was a faster method, but not as sturdy. Weavers often decorated finished baskets with animal designs or tribal symbols. They used plant dyes to color the materials shades of red, yellow, black, purple, green-blue, brown, and white. They also used feathers, quills, shells, leather, or beads as decorations. Size varied from small **trinket** baskets to storage jars over 4 feet (1 meter) high, which could take as long as two years to make.

TEXTILES

Fabric weaving is a lot like basket weaving, since it consists of threading strips of one material over and under stiffer strips of another material. However, preparing the materials is difficult, and it took thousands of years longer to develop. By AD 700, the Anasazi had developed a simple upright loom. It was a large square made of wooden poles that held the stiffer fibers in place. The cloth that they wove from cactus fiber and hemp plants resembles the cotton that is woven today. It was used to make blankets, **serapes**, shawls, shoes, and bags. Because **sacred** symbols and designs were woven into the fabrics, weaving was considered a sacred job. Women—and in some cultures, men—were considered the weavers of the thread of life.

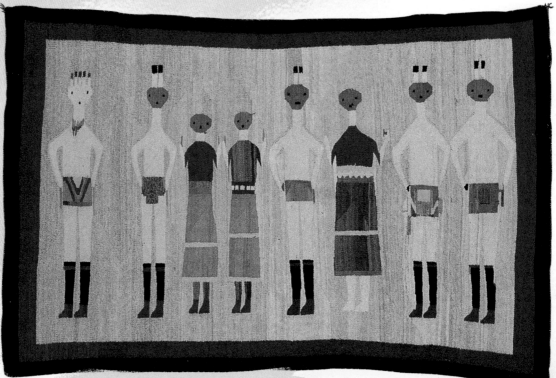

Navajo blanket, Navajo people, Arizona, wool

Navajo blankets are still woven on looms made by the weaver.

Chilkat weave shirt, Tlingit people, Alaska, cedar bark and mountain goat wool weave with fur lining

The chilkat weave symbolized wealth. Sometimes wealthy people burned these shirts and robes as proof of their wealth and status.

Weaving materials

In addition to plant fibers, weavers used feathers and the fur of animals such as rabbits and dogs. The weaving of wool did not begin until the Spanish introduced sheep into the Southwest culture area around AD 1600. Other popular sources of weaving materials used after European settlers arrived included the old uniforms, army blankets, and red flannel underwear that settlers traded to Native Americans. The Native Americans unraveled these items and re-dyed the wool. They then wove it into their own designs to make blankets and clothing.

POTTERY

The first **nomadic** Native Americans used lightweight baskets to gather and store food. Pottery developed much later, when people discovered that if they smeared baskets with clay and then dried them, the baskets would hold water. By the year 200 BC, the Hohokam people of the Southwest culture area were molding bowls and jars out of wet clay. Potters' wheels did not exist until Europeans introduced them in the 1500s. Instead, a potter would use the bottom of a broken pot to form the base of a new one. He or she rolled coils of clay to form the walls of the bowl or jug, then pinched the coils together, shaped the pot with tools made from gourds or sticks, and smoothed water over it. The potter hardened pottery over an outdoor fire, often using dried animal dung for fuel.

This pottery was found in Mesa Verde, an Anasazi city built high on the cliffs of Colorado.

Pottery, Anasazi people, Mesa Verde, Colorado, c. AD 600–1300

By AD 700, people in the Southwest culture area were painting their pottery in striking black-and-white designs. The artists chewed the ends of twigs to make their brushes. They also began making small, animal-shaped ceremonial figures and pipes out of clay. Over time, individual villages became known for their different pot shapes and decorative styles, which included animal and insect shapes and geometric patterns. Yellow and red became the traditional colors in some areas, while other cultures continued to use black and white.

Pot with bat, Mogollon people, Gila Cliff Dwellings, New Mexico, c. AD 950–1350

This pot was made to be used in a burial. We can tell that it was never used, since it does not have a hole in the bottom.

With the exception of some parts of the Northwest Pacific Coast culture area, pottery developed all over North America. It was never as beautifully shaped and painted in other places as it was in the Southwest, however.

Mimbres burial pottery

Pottery also played a major role in religious ceremonies and rituals. When **archaeologists** excavated (uncovered) the Mogollon people's burial sites in the Mimbres area, they discovered skeletal remains with clay bowls covering the heads. Magical images of clouds, animals, and spirits were painted on the inside of each bowl. Each bowl had a hole in the bottom so that the person's spirit could escape.

JEWELRY AND HEADDRESSES

Many Native North Americans wore some type of jewelry or other body decoration to show that they belonged to a certain **clan** or tribe. The jewelry was often a tooth, claw, or other animal part carried as a totem, or it was an amulet, hair ornament, or necklace made out of beads, shells, or feathers. Such items were often given to teenagers to celebrate their passage into adulthood after their vision quest, or to young men when they became warriors. Beads and feathers also decorated clothing worn to celebrate weddings or other special ceremonies. Necklaces made of shells were worn to prevent illness, and shamans often wore red face paint and red hair ornaments to cure a sickness.

Disk with crested woodpeckers, shell, c. AD 1250–1300

This disk was carved to decorate a necklace. The woodpeckers carved on it would have had great importance for the owner.

Native Americans added glass beads to their jewelry and clothing designs after Europeans introduced them to North America in the 1500s. In some cultures, men and women wore **wampum** beads to show they were important tribal members. The beads were also used as money to trade for other goods.

Many Native American cultures also came to be known for their featherwork. People wore feathers as jewelry or on clothing and headdresses to mark their social status, and some feathers were worn in spiritual ceremonies. One common belief was that a feather represented the qualities of the bird it came from. Cherokee tribes considered owl, hummingbird, eagle, turkey, and buzzard feathers particularly powerful. They believed that owl feathers represented wisdom, while eagle feathers represented honor and success.

Warbonnet, Arapaho people, eagle feathers, shells, beads, and leather

Warbonnets like this one were worn by tribes that lived on the Plains. This bonnet is fairly short. Some of them had feathers that reached all the way down to the wearer's knees!

SAND PAINTINGS

According to Navajo legend, Holy People animate (give spirit or life to) all things, including animals, people, trees, winds, rivers, and even colors and the four directions. The Holy People teach about the harmony of the universe. The Navajo believe that to keep the Holy People happy, everything must be kept in balance. When a Navajo is sick or has misfortune, it is because bad spirits have entered his or her body, and he or she has thrown the balance of the universe out of harmony. To regain health or fortune, the person must ask an *Hatathli*, which means "Singer," to conduct a long and complex healing ceremony. An important part of this ceremony is the creation of sand paintings.

This modern Navajo shaman is creating a sand painting for a healing ceremony.

The Singer is the Navajo shaman. He or she uses colored sand to create a sacred design on a large piece of **buckskin**.

Then the sick person is purified with sweat baths. This means that he or she is placed in a small, covered place where a fire is burning, making the area full of steam. The steam makes the person sweat all of the bad things out of his or her body.

After this, the person kneels in the middle of the painting, facing east, and prays, often for days at a time, while the Singer chants. The colors white, blue, yellow, and black symbolize dawn, daylight, twilight, and night. The Singer draws the spirits of animals and draws plants, such as corn, beans, squash, and tobacco, that have special healing powers. When the healing ritual is over, the painting is swept away. The healing ceremony and sand painting are ancient traditions. They have been important ceremonies in the Navajo culture for hundreds of years.

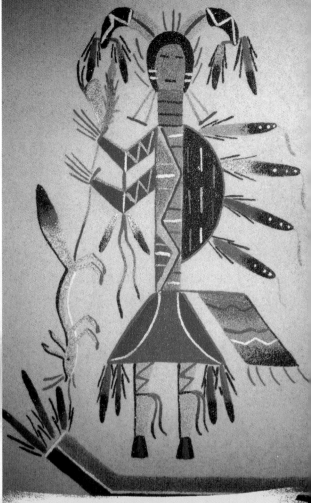

Sand painting of a Yei God, Navajo shaman, western New Mexico, colored sand, c. AD 1985–1995

Yei gods, like the one in this painting, are summoned by shamans to cure a sick person by pushing the bad spirits out of his or her body.

Bear sickness
The Navajo believe that feeling faint, feeling nervous, and having troubled memory are all symptoms of a condition called bear sickness. This sickness can be caused by eating bear meat, killing a bear, or dreaming about a bear. To cure bear sickness, the shaman makes a sand painting and performs a ceremony called the Mountain Chant, or Mountaintop Way.

EARTH MOUNDS

Some of the most impressive Native American creations archaeologists have discovered are the more than 100,000 **earth mounds** found throughout the Eastern Woodlands culture area and in the Ohio and Mississippi River valleys. Many are small, simple mounds, but others are huge works of art that are built in the shape of birds or animals. Some are as large as the Great Pyramids of Egypt. They can only be fully appreciated when they are viewed from the air. The Great Serpent Mound in Ohio is 1,348 feet long, 20 feet wide, and 2½ feet high (410 meters long, 6 meters wide, and 80 centimeters high).

Some scientists think that the serpent mound was designed as a ceremonial calendar.

Great Serpent Mound, Adena people, sculpted mound of soil and rock, near Locust Grove, Ohio, c. 100 BC to AD 700

Panorama of the Monumental Grandeur of the Mississippi Valley, *John J. Egan, c.* AD *1850*

This painting shows archaeologists studying an earth mound in the Mississippi River Valley.

It is likely that the mounds were built over a span of several thousand years, from about 700 BC to about AD 1500, by three main farming cultures: the Adena, the Hopewell, and the Mississippian (also called the Natchez). Most mounds were built as burial monuments and had a central chamber that contained the remains of important tribal members. Others were cemetery plots for less important people, often containing 50 or more separately buried bodies. New mounds were often built on top of older ones from previous generations.

Objects that were buried with the dead, including pottery, effigy pipes, and tools, were often made from materials such as copper, seashells, and certain kinds of stone that were not readily available in the Eastern Woodlands. This tells archaeologists that the mound-building cultures must have traded over great distances with people from other culture areas.

NATIVE AMERICAN PAINTING

For thousands of years, Native American artists painted rocks, pottery, and leather objects with images that reflected their spiritual beliefs, community history, and pride. In the 1800s and early 1900s, Native Americans were forced to give up their culture so that they could blend in with white Americans. As a result, many Native American art forms disappeared. By the 1950s, institutions such as the Institute of American Indian Art began to encourage Native American artists to go back and relearn their traditional art forms. Today the nation's most important artists include Native Americans such as Juane Quick-to-See Smith. These modern artists are using traditional and sacred art forms to express new ideas.

> In this painting, Smith has drawn outlines of a traditional image—the buffalo—over a collage made of articles and pictures that illustrate the selfish qualities of modern society.

Herd, *Juane Quick-to-See Smith, 1998*

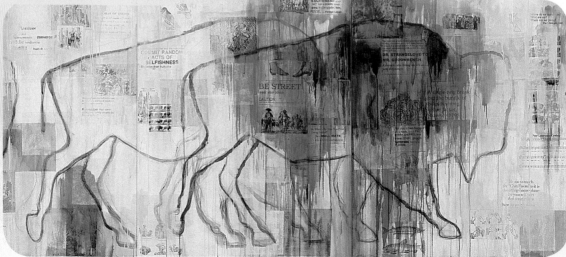

Make a buckskin painting

Materials:

- **Strong brown paper, cut into a large rectangle**
- **Crayons in colors like brown, orange, red, black, and yellow**
- **Newspapers**
- **An iron**
- **Black permanent marker**
- **Wax furniture polish**

1. Use the crayons to draw an image on the paper. Use the painting on page 5 for guidance. When your drawing is finished, rub the wax over all the areas of the paper that are not covered in crayon.

2. Crush the paper with your picture on it into a ball, then open it up again. Repeat this about twenty times to make your picture look old and wrinkled. You can even step on the ball to make the wrinkles deeper.

3. Put your open picture between two layers of newspaper. Have an adult help you iron the newspaper above your picture until the wax begins to melt through the newspaper.

4. Remove your picture from the newspaper and go over the outlines in black permanent marker. Cut the picture into the shape of an animal hide (skin). Your picture should have the wrinkled look and soft feel of a real buckskin painting.

TIMELINE

BC

50,000 to 15,000	The first migration across the Bering Strait brings people to North America.
10,000	The first stone arrowheads are carved in the Great Plains.
9000	Basketry and early woodcarving are developed throughout North America.
4000	Early weaving techniques are developed and used to make baskets.
2000	Painted pottery develops in the Southwest.
500	The Anasazi and Plains people start creating rock art.
700	Cultures in the Eastern Woodlands culture area and Ohio and Mississippi River valleys start building earth mounds.

AD

1492	Christopher Columbus establishes the first European colony in North America.
1500s	Europeans introduce the potter's wheel, the upright loom, beads, and metalwork to some Native American cultures.
1800s	Congress passes the Indian Removal Act, forcing Native Americans onto reservations (areas of land set aside by the U.S. government).
1880–1890s	U.S. troops in the West kill many Native Americans who are fighting to keep their land.
1940	Juane Quick-to-See Smith is born.
1950s	Native American artists relearn old pottery, weaving, carving, and basketry skills as a result of the founding of the Institute of American Indian Art.
1989	The National Museum of the American Indian is established by an act of Congress.
1990	The Indian Arts and Crafts Act is passed, and all authentic Native American art is certified (recognized as authentic).

FIND OUT MORE

You can find out more about Native American art in books and on the Internet. Use a search engine such as www.yahooligans.com to search for information. A search for the words "Native American art" will bring back lots of results, but it may be difficult to find the information you want. Try refining your search to look for some of the ideas mentioned in this book, such as "sand painting."

More books to read
January, Brendan. *Native Americans*. Chicago: Raintree, 2005
Murdoch, David. *Eyewitness: North American Indian*. New York: Dorling Kindersley, 2005.

GLOSSARY

amulet ornament carried to protect the wearer

ancestor person you are related to from the past, such as your grandmother

archaeologist person who studies the past using objects made by people in the past

buckskin tanned deer hide (skin) used to make clothing, tents, and other objects

ceremonial used in a ritual

clan group of people with something in common, who usually live together

culture area region of the United States where there were several Native American groups that shared beliefs and customs

earth mound massive burial site that was often built in an animal shape

effigy pipe pipe carved to resemble a person or animal spirit

functional made to use in everyday life, or as part of religious ceremonies

limestone soft stone that is easy to carve

nomadic tending to move from place to place

petroglyph picture carved into rock to tell a story

pictograph painting on rock

pipestone soft, red stone, also called catlinite, that was used to make pipes

potlatch elaborate feast common in the Northwest Pacific Coast area

rattle musical instrument that makes noise when it is shaken

sacred highly respected or worshiped

sacrifice losing or giving away something important for the good of others

serape woven cape worn over the shoulders

shaman Native American religious leader who can communicate with the spirits

spiritual to do with religion

totem animal spirit used as a family symbol and as personal protection

trinket small object

vision quest spiritual journey made by young Native Americans to mark the change from childhood to adulthood

wampum beads made of shells or other valuable materials that were worn and also used as money

wigwam round shelter made of poles and covered with bark or hides

Index